EUREKA! DETAILS TO FOLLOW

CARTOONS ON CHEMISTRY

by SIDNEY HARRIS

Harris, Sidney.
EUREKA! DETAILS TO FOLLOW
Cartoons on Chemistry

ISBN 978-0-9890685-1-2

Most of the cartoons in this book have been previously published, and appeared in following magazines: *American Scientist, Bulletin of the Atomic Scientists, Chronicle of Higher Education, Clinical Chemistry News, Environment, Fantasy and Science Fiction, Harvard Business Review, JohnsHopkins Magazine, Playboy, Science, Science 80, The Scientist, Today's Chemist at Work, U.S Medicine, W.P.I. Journal*

Sidney Harris
Box 1980, Federal Station
New Haven, CT 06521
USA

Or

sharris777@aol.com
ScienceCartoonsPlus.com

Book layout and logo design by Martha Bradshaw

BOOKS BY THE SAME AUTHOR:

So Far, So Good

Pardon Me, Miss

What's So Funny About Science?

What's So Funny About Computers?

What's So Funny About Business?

All Ends Up

Chicken Soup, and Other Medical Matters

Einstein Simplified

Science Goes To the Dogs

Can't You Guys Read?

So Sue Me

Stress Test

Freudian Slips

Chalk Up Another One

Einstein Atomized

You Want Proof? I'll Give You Proof

From Personal Ads to Cloning Labs

There Goes the Neighborhood

The Interactive Toaster

There Goes Archimedes

At Home With the Einsteins

49 Dogs, 36 Cats and a Platypus

101 Funny Things About Global Warming

ASIDE FROM THE COCKROACH, how was everything?

Cartoons on THE DANGERS OF EATING

Foreword

When I taught chemistry, I spiced up my lectures with jokes such as these:

Why do chemists call helium, curium, and barium the medical elements?
Because if you can't helium or curium, you've got to barium!
What would you call a clown who's in jail? A silicon!

When I told my department head that I could earn a living telling jokes such as these, he advised me not to quit my day job!

Here's a description of Sidney Harris's day job: Most mornings, Sidney climbs the stairs to the upper floor of his home and cogitates for about four hours. He primes his creative pump by reading broadly, culling the essence of a scientific concept and then allowing it to ricochet between the left and right hemispheres of his brain.

Like a fisherman who casts bait all morning hoping to catch a big one, more mornings than not, Sidney lands a big one and descends with his latest catch, another delightful cartoon. Not a bad day job, eh?

His humor, like all humor, arises from the unexpected and the incongruous. It surprises us into a new point of view. Appreciation of humor, however, requires sufficient background and insight in order to recognize something as unexpected or incongruous.

Thus, each cartoon is a test of scientific literacy. To "get" the joke, the reader must possess a basic understanding of its subject matter.

What's so funny about potassium nitrate?
What's so funny about cyclic aliphatic hydrocarbons?
What's so funny about the periodic table?

If you don't get the joke, the fault is not Sidney's.
Get ready to have fun testing your scientific literacy by answering the question: *What's so funny about chemistry?*

Enjoy!

Charles M. Wynn, Sr., Ph.D.
Professor of Chemistry Emeritus
Eastern Connecticut State University

This book is dedicated to Jane V. Olson (1916-2006), the wonderful editor of American Scientist, who encouraged me to do cartoons about science.

"I'VE DONE SOME PRIVATE RESEARCH, AND IT APPEARS I'M RECEIVING THE MINIMUM WAGE FOR A NOBEL-PRIZE WINNER."

"NOT ONLY PHARMACEUTICALS — WE'RE ALSO FINDING ALL SORTS OF INDUSTRIAL CHEMICALS HERE."

"JUST BECAUSE THE ALIGNMENT OF THE SYSTEM WASN'T MAINTAINED DURING RAPID SAMPLE EXCHANGE, IT'S NO THREAT TO YOUR MANHOOD."

THE VENN-DIAGRAM BUILDINGS

BIOLOGY
+ CHEMISTRY & PHYSICS
& A LITTLE PHYSICAL CHEMISTRY

CHEMISTRY
+ BIOLOGY & PHYSICS
& A LITTLE BIOPHYSICS

PHYSICS
+ BIOLOGY & CHEMISTRY
& A LITTLE BIOCHEMISTRY

S.Harris

LAB SAFETY RULE NO. 1...

DO NOT DRINK SUBSTANCES TO DETERMINE
IF THEY ARE POISONOUS

SPECTROMETER BLUES

Woke up this mornin',
Found my prism cloudy 'n cracked.
Just as the day was dawnin'
All my nerves felt torn 'n wracked.

Baseline's elevated,
Can't get it under control.
Photomultiplier's saturated,
Nothin but mis'ry in my soul.
From infrared to UV blues,
My spectrometer's bad news...

"MR. NEWTON, WE HAVE CAREFULLY REVIEWED YOUR WORK IN ALCHEMY,
AND HAVE COME TO ONE CONCLUSION: STICK TO PHYSICS."

"OF COURSE YOU CAN'T REPLICATE MY EXPERIMENTS. THAT'S THE BEAUTY OF THEM."

"CAUTION: THIS TOMATO SOUP COMBINED WITH OUR CHICKEN NOODLE SOUP CAN FORM A LETHAL NERVE GAS."

"DON'T MIND ASHLEY. AFTER LOOKING THROUGH A MICROSCOPE ALL DAY, ANYTHING LARGE STARTLES HIM."

BREAKTHROUGH BY A COMIC

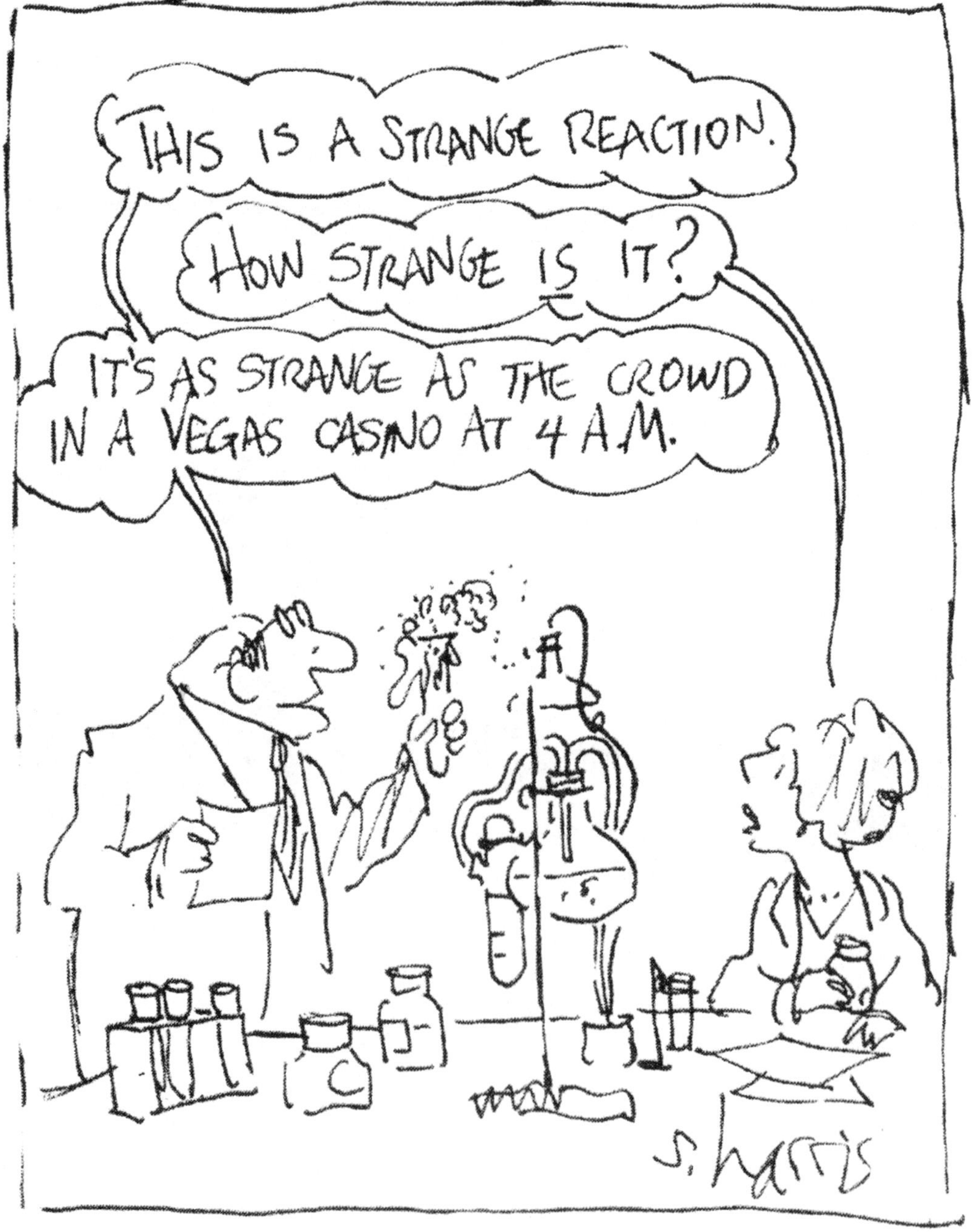

"ESSENTIALLY WILKINS PROVES THINGS AND BRENNER DISPROVES THEM."

"SEE— IT WORKS IN MY FANTASY RESEARCH LEAGUE."

"HE'S WRITING HIS MEMOIRS. I BELIEVE HE'S UP TO CYCLIC ALIPHATIC HYDROCARBONS."

FRONT Row, L. to R.: Organic, Pharmacology, Polymer, Inorganic, Agrochemical
BACK Row: Analytical, Radiochemical, Environmental, Biochem, Industrial

"SURPRISINGLY ENOUGH, THIS IS IN THE RANGE OF ACCEPTABLE RISK."

"I CAN HELP YOU WITH TINY, LITTLE STEPS. AS FOR BREAKTHROUGHS, YOU'RE ON YOUR OWN."

GREAT MOMENTS IN SHOPPING

LOUIS PASTEUR BUYING HIS FIRST
QUART OF PASTEURIZED MILK

"SCIENCE FRAUD! WHAT DO I DO THAT ISN'T SCIENCE FRAUD?"

"FORGET ABOUT IT. YOUR PEAK BREAKTHROUGH YEARS WERE YOUR TWENTIES."

"...AND THE WOMEN WHO USED THE PLACEBO MAKEUP TURNED OUT TO BE JUST AS ATTRACTIVE."

"THE CODEINE IS O.K. AND THE PHENOBARBITAL IS O.K., BUT THE F.D.A. SAYS NO TO THE POWDERED BAT'S TOOTH."

"I KNOW PASTEUR DIDN'T WORK UNDER THESE CONDITIONS, BUT PASTEUR DIDN'T HAVE FIFTY COMPANIES TRYING TO STEAL HIS TRADE SECRETS."

"FOXCROFT, YOUR RESEARCH ON THE IMMUNE SYSTEM, AND THE DRUGS YOU'VE COME UP WITH ARE EXTRAORDINARY. AS A RESULT, WE'RE MAKING YOU A DISTRICT SALES MANAGER."

THOUGH HE CREATED MORE THAN
300 PRODUCTS FROM PEANUTS, GEORGE
WASHINGTON CARVER WAS UNABLE TO
CHANGE EVEN ONE OF THEM BACK INTO
A PEANUT

"I THOUGHT HE WOULD RUN ALL SORTS OF SCIENTIFIC TESTS."

"I THOUGHT IT WAS ALL SCIENCESPEAK, BUT IT TURNS OUT BIOSPEAK IS NOTHING LIKE CHEMSPEAK."

THE OLD SCIENTIFIC METHOD

THE NEW SCIENTIFIC METHOD

"UNFORTUNATELY THIS LAB IS FUNDED ONLY BY AS MUCH GOLD AS WE CAN MAKE FROM LEAD."

"THOSE CONSTANTLY CHANGING GOVERNMENT REGULATIONS — NOW THEY SAY MY DESK IS SEVEN INCHES TOO LONG."

"THE STATISTICIAN IS COMING OVER TO EXPLAIN WHY THIS IS PERFECTLY NORMAL.

"I'D LIKE TO KNOW WHY WE'RE SELLING ELEMENTS TO THESE COMPANIES, AND THEN TURN AROUND AND BUY COMPOUNDS FROM THEM."

"IF I LEARNED ONE THING IN ALL MY YEARS IN THIS BUSINESS, IT'S THAT YOU'RE ONLY AS GOOD AS YOUR LAST EARTHSHAKING BREAKTHROUGH."

"IF ONLY THERE WAS SOME PEACEFUL USE FOR NERVE GAS."

"IF WE WERE IN THE RENAISSANCE, WE'D BE
PAINTING NATIVITY SCENES RIGHT NOW."

"IT APPEARS TO BE A MAJOR BREAKTHROUGH, BUT THAT WOULD BE IMPOSSIBLE — HE DOESN'T HAVE A PH.D."

"IT MAY VERY WELL BRING ABOUT IMMORTALITY, BUT
IT WILL TAKE FOREVER TO TEST IT."

"IT STARTED WITH A SIMPLE CASE OF PEER-REVIEW."

"I'VE NEVER FELT BETTER SINCE I
FELL INTO THAT VAT OF ANTIBIOTICS."

"DON'T FORGET—KEEP THE POTASSIUM CHLORIDE IN A SEPARATE CONTAINER."

"I'M ON THE VERGE OF A MAJOR BREAKTHROUGH, BUT I'M ALSO AT THAT POINT WHERE CHEMISTRY LEAVES OFF AND PHYSICS BEGINS, SO I'LL HAVE TO DROP THE WHOLE THING."

"WE JUST DON'T GET INVOLVED WITH THINGS LIKE DOUBLE-BLIND TESTS AND PEER REVIEW. WE'RE JUST A LITTLE MOM-AND-POP LABORATORY."

"IT'S NOT THE HEAT <u>OR</u> THE HUMIDITY. IT'S THE SULFUR DIOXIDE, HYDROGEN SULFIDE, NON-METHANE HYDROCARBONS AND SULFURIC ACID MIST."

"WE'LL HAVE TO RETRACT THAT ARTICLE. ONE OF OUR CO-AUTHORS IS THE NIGHT WATCHMAN."

"I'M SURE YOU KNOW THAT THIS IS IN CONFLICT WITH SEVERAL RELIGIOUS BELIEFS."

"WELL, WELL — THIS SHOULD CREATE A NICE LITTLE WAVE OF PANIC AND HYSTERIA."

"OH, YEAH! I'VE FORGOTTEN MORE ABOUT ANIOMIC POLYMERIZATION IN MOLECULAR ADSORBATES AT INTERFACES THROUGH ION CHROMATOGRAPHY, THERMAL ANALYSIS AND UV SPECTROPHOTOMETRY FOR FORMULATION OF PROCESS DEVELOPMENT THAN YOU'LL EVER KNOW."

"AFTER ALL THESE YEARS, I'M SURE OF ONLY ONE THING:
WHEN I HEAT THE LIQUID IT BOILS."

"WE'VE REALLY COME UP WITH SOMETHING, BUT NINE OTHER LABS ALSO CAME UP WITH IT THIS WEEK."

"AND YET THE BUILDING IS CONCRETE, THE TANKS
ARE METAL, THE WINDOWS ARE GLASS..."

PERIODIC TABLE AND
AVOIRDUPOIS WEIGHT OF THE
MENDELEEV FAMILY

"WHAT AUSTRIAN BIO-CHEMIST IS WASTING HIS TIME WITH FALSE ANTI-BODY LEADS?' SAY—OUR JOURNAL HAS A GOSSIP COLUMN!"

"SIMPLE. YOU FORGOT TO ADD
THE POTASSIUM NITRATE."

"WHAT DO YOU EXPECT, SINCE 90% OF ALL THE SCIENTISTS WHO EVER LIVED ARE ALIVE TODAY."

LOUIS PASTEUR TELLS A JOKE...

HIPPOCRATES, TWO ALCHEMISTS, MARIE CURIE'S UNCLE, THREE WINEMAKERS, LAVOISIER, ARISTOTLE AND A TEN·YEAR·OLD BOY ARE BEING CHASED BY A MAD DOG DOWN A STREET IN AVIGNON...

I'm your guardian angel, and I think it's time you knew that for the past 37 years you've been barking up the wrong tree.
S. Harris

Research Hand Signals

This is going to take about nine years

I think I'm on to something

We need another #3 million

"THE FUNNY THING IS, OUR WASTES ARE PERFECTLY HARMLESS."

"WHY SHOULD I BE HAPPY? I COME HERE EVERY DAY AND KNOCK MYSELF OUT, AND THEY GIVE ME A NOBEL PRIZE FOR SOMETHING I DID WHEN I WAS 27 YEARS OLD."

"...THEN - AND HERE'S THE FUNNY PART—
I ADD THE POTASSIUM SULFATE..."

"YOU HAVE TO BELIEVE WHAT YOU'RE DOING WILL LEAD TO SOMETHING VALUABLE, EVEN THOUGH IT PROBABLY WON'T."

"IT'S THE LATEST FABRIC: 40% DACRON, 40% ORLON, 20% RECOMBINANT DNA."

"THIS LOVELY OLD SONG TELLS OF A YOUNG WOMAN WHO LEAVES HER LITTLE COTTAGE, AND GOES OFF TO WORK. SHE ARRIVES AT HER DESTINATION WHERE SHE PLACES SOME SOLID NH_4HS IN A FLASK CONTAINING 0.50 ATM OF AMMONIA, AND TRIES TO DETERMINE THE PRESSURES OF AMMONIA AND HYDROGEN SULFIDE WHEN EQUILIBRIUM IS REACHED."

"WHY, IT'S CHEMISTRY, COMING UP THE RIVER FROM NEW ORLEANS."

AFTER ANTOINE LAVOISIER DISCOVERED
OXYGEN, HIS WHOLE FAMILY WOULD BREATHE IT
REGULARLY AS A SHOW OF SUPPORT

DMITRI IVANOVICH MENDELEEV (1834-1907)

AT THE ST. PETERSBURG CONFERENCE, FOUR OF MY
COLLEAGUES WERE STANDING SIDE BY SIDE.
  KOSYK WEIGHED 140 POUNDS, PETROVNA WEIGHED 160,
SHABELSKY WEIGHED 180 AND LEBEDEV 200.

"HMMM..." I THOUGHT...

"ALTHOUGH YOUR DISCOVERY IS VERY IMPORTANT, THE CONSENSUS IS THAT YOUR ARTICLE ABOUT IT LACKED SUSPENSE, AND WAS COMPLETELY DEVOID OF HUMOR."

"IT'S WHAT THE PEOPLE WANT. YOU RUN WILD FOR A COUPLE OF HOURS AND THEN — ZAP! — YOU'RE BACK TO NORMAL."

"BUT YOU BOTH CAN'T BE THE 'FATHER' OF
AMMONIUM PENTOXIDE PHOSPHATE."

"THEN WE'LL JUST MARK IT
'DO NOT SHAKE WELL BEFORE USING'."

"THEY'RE VERY PROUD OF ME. I'M THE FIRST ONE IN THE FAMILY TO BECOME A BIOMOLECULAR PHARMOKINETIC INTEGRATIVE-TOXICOLOGICAL MULTIPHOTON-IMAGING PHENOTYPIC ANALYST."

"THEY CLAIM YOUR PAPER WAS WRITTEN BY A GHOST WRITER AND YOUR RESEARCH WAS DONE BY A GHOST SCIENTIST."

"BUT FREDRICK, IT'S NINE YEARS SINCE YOUR BREAKTHROUGH. YOU CAN'T JUST DO NOTHING UNTIL THE WORLD RECOGNIZES YOU."

"HOW'S THE NEW INSOMNIA PILL GOING?"

"...BUT OUR MOST USEFUL PUBLICATION IS THE 'JOURNAL OF DON'T-DO-IT: IT'S-ALREADY-BEEN-DONE'."

"IN OTHER WORDS, IT BREAKS LARGE
MOLECULES INTO SMALL ONES."

"ACCORDING TO THESE LATEST TESTS, ANYTHING CAN CAUSE ANYTHING."

"BELIEVE ME, YOU NEVER LOOKED BETTER SINCE YOU FELL INTO THAT VAT OF SKIN CREAM."

"REPORT CARDS, FOLKS — AND THEY HAVE TO BE SIGNED BY YOUR HIGH SCHOOL CHEMISTRY TEACHERS."

"THEREFORE, WHEN IT BURSTS, THE BUBBLE GUM WILL NOT STICK TO YOUR NOSE."

"I'M ATTEMPTING TO TRANSMUTE CALCIUM OXIDE, COPPER GLUCONATE, MANGANESE SULFATE, TYROSINE AND BENZALDEHYDE INTO CONDENSED SOUP."

AUGUSTE ESCOFFIER AND LOUIS PASTEUR

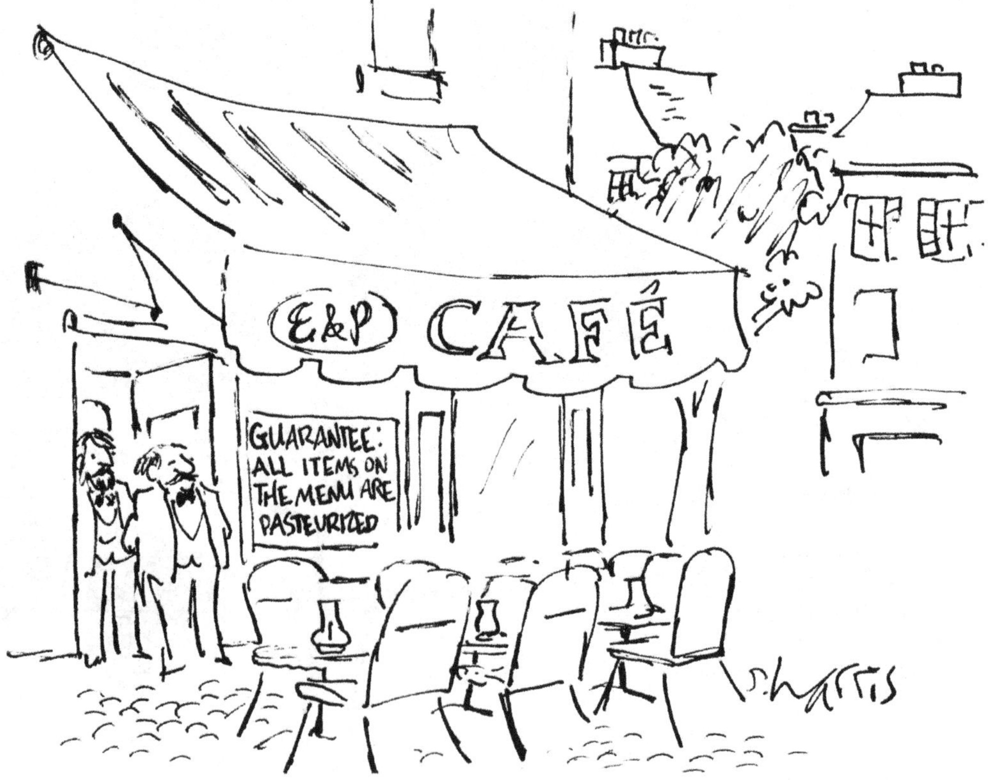

"ALL WE WANT IS A NON-LETHAL GAS THAT WILL MAKE THE ENEMY FEEL FRIENDLY TOWARDS US, LAY DOWN THEIR ARMS, AND JOIN US IN A SPIRIT OF BROTHERHOOD."

"YOU MUST ADMIT THAT CHOCOLATE COVERED HAZARDOUS WASTES ARE BETTER THAN PLAIN HAZARDOUS WASTES."

"FREEZE! WE'RE TAKING A LOOK AT YOUR ADDITIVES, PRESERVATIVES, ARTIFICIAL COLORING..."

"A GOOD IDEA, LOUIS, BUT MAYBE YOU CAN 'PASTEURIZE' SOMETHING BESIDES PAINT."

"BUT IF HE'S RIGHT, IT'LL SAVE US YEARS OF EXPERIMENTING."

"HE'S FALSIFIED DATA, HE'S FALSIFIED RESULTS...
AND NOW HE SAYS HE LOVES ME."

"SOME CLEAN ROOM — THERE'S A FLY IN MY POTASSIUM NITRATE."

"THE BOTTOM LINE: DO WE WAIT FOR THE GOVERNMENT TO APPROVE IT AS AN ANTIBIOTIC, OR DO WE GO AHEAD RIGHT NOW AND SELL IT AS A FURNITURE POLISH?"

"EVERY TIME I COME UP WITH SOMETHING IT TURNS OUT TO BE ASPIRIN."

'WE HOPE TO MAKE ANTIBIOTICS, INTERFERON AND DIAGNOSTIC PRODUCTS, BUT JUST TO BE ON THE SAFE SIDE, WE'RE STARTING OUT WITH A LINE OF SHAMPOOS.'

"DID YOU HEAR THAT MARKETING WANTS US TO MOVE INTO 'COMPRESSED LIQUIDS' NEXT?"

Made in the USA
Columbia, SC
23 November 2018